Jesus and Peter

Jesus and Peter

Off-the-record conversations

John L. Bell
Graham Maule

WILD GOOSE PUBLICATIONS
THE IONA COMMUNITY

First published 1999
Reprinted 2004

ISBN 1 901557 17 0

Copyright © 1999 Wild Goose Resource Group

Front cover: Graham Maule © Wild Goose Resource Group

The authors have asserted their rights under the Copyright, Designs and
Patents Act 1988, to be identified as the authors of this work.

Published by Wild Goose Publications
4th Floor, Savoy House, 140 Sauchiehall Street,
Glasgow G2 3DH
– the publishing division of the Iona Community.
Scottish Charity No. SCO03794. Limited Company Reg.No. SCO96243.

The Wild Goose is a Celtic symbol of the Holy Spirit.
It is the trademark of Wild Goose Publications.

Extracts which appear from The Revised English Bible and
The Good News Bible are used with permission.
Revised English Bible © Oxford University Press & Cambridge University Press
Good News Bible published by The Bible Societies / HarperCollins
Publishers Ltd UK © American Bible Society, 1966, 1971, 1976, 1992

Overseas distribution:
Australia: Willow Connection Pty Ltd, Unit 4A,
3-9 Kenneth Road, Manly Vale, NSW 2093.
New Zealand: Pleroma, Higginson Street, Otane 4170,
Central Hawkes Bay.
Permission to reproduce any part of this work in Australia or New
Zealand should be sought from Willow Connection.

A catalogue record for this book is available from the British Library.

Produced by Reliance Production Company, Hong Kong
Printed and bound in China

Contents

Introduction

Years ago, we published a small collection of Jesus and Peter dialogues, soon followed by a second and third. The reception given to these conversations between Christ and his eager disciple was both a surprise and a great encouragement.

The scripts have all emerged from specific contexts where we have been asked to lead worship. These include national events (Christian Aid conferences, Greenbelt festivals, etc.), regional initiatives (such as Last Night Out, a monthly event we run in Glasgow) and local congregational worship.

Since then the conversations have been read sometimes in small groups, sometimes in Sunday morning services, sometimes as discussion starters for a confirmation class. Some people have even read them on their way home on the bus.

Within the pages of this collection you'll find twenty-four scripts: seventeen of them have been previously printed but have been revised and there are seven which are published here for the first time. Most are dialogues, with the exception of *Table talk*, which includes all the disciples (and can be used as a preface to Holy Communion); *What is Caesar's?*, which features the two Zealots, Judas and Simon; and *The denial*, which is a monologue by Peter for Maundy Thursday.

You'll also find biblical passages before each script. We have included these with the intention of providing a context and reference point, rather than for reading immediately before the dialogue. Occasionally, this might be appropriate, but more often than not will be unnecessary. Sometimes reading the passage may even defeat the purpose of reading the script.

We have arranged the contents of the book in a (roughly) chronological order, following Jesus' life from the beginning of his ministry in Galilee; through his parables and miracles; his teaching of the disciples; his approach to and entry into Jerusalem; through Holy Week to Easter Day and beyond. We hope this aids your selection of the scripts, whether you are using them as part of a study series or for a particular act of worship in a particular liturgical season.

You should feel at liberty to change expressions which do not seem natural in your part of the world. The recurrent words 'Eh ... Jesus' may in some places be better replaced by 'Emm ...' or 'Umm ...' or 'Hey ...'. Where occasionally a script contains a particularly Scottish word or phrase, the English equivalent is given beside it in brackets. Our intention has never been that Jesus and the disciples should speak only with Glasgow accents.

And while West of Scotland accents are not a prerequisite to the reading of these exchanges, there are some dos (or more accurately don'ts) that should be taken into account. Take a moment to read the section 'How *not* to use these scripts' overleaf before giving voice to the carpenter and the fisherman.

John L. Bell
Graham Maule

How *not* to use these scripts

1. Get a priest or minister. Dress him in clerical gear with academic hood and ask him to read the part of Jesus.

   and

2. Get a man who has a blue polo neck or smock to cover himself with fish scales and read the part of Peter.

   or

3. Recruit two people who do amateur dramatics, especially those who can't understand why they never made the West End or Broadway.

4. Never ask a girl or a woman to read a part. They might get emotional.

5. Don't let anyone read who is too young. Remember that Jesus and his disciples must have been respectably middle-aged.

6. Ensure that whoever reads has received pronunciation. We can't have people thinking that Jesus and Peter spoke with a regional accent!

7. Get the Jesus reader to stand in the pulpit and Peter at the lectern, so that everyone can see who is more important.

8. Make sure the parts are memorised and that the readers act them out, making the occasional theatrical gesture to emphasise the point.

9. Have something appropriate played on the organ before and after. Bach has a lot of nice wee preludes which would do.

10. Discourage any reaction from the congregation. In fact, make an announcement before the script is used to prohibit anyone laughing.

How *really* to use these scripts

Disregard everything said overleaf. Don't enact unless you must, but get someone to listen critically while you rehearse in situ what you are going to read, and pause now and then when it seems appropriate.

The call

As Jesus walked along the shore of the Lake of Galilee, he saw two brothers, Simon (called Peter) and his brother Andrew, casting a net into the lake; for they were fishermen.

Matthew 4: 18

The two characters stand apart from each other, Peter looking quite absorbed in himself.

Personnel: **Jesus**
              Peter

Jesus: Peter ... ?

Peter: Yes, Jesus ... ?

Jesus: Come with me.

Peter: Where are you going?

Jesus: I'm not telling you.

Peter: Do you not know?

Jesus: Oh yes, I've a fair idea.

Peter: Then ... why won't you tell me?

Jesus: You might not like it.

Peter: Well, thanks for your consideration, Jesus.

(A pause)

Jesus: Peter … ?

Peter: Yes, Jesus … ?

Jesus: Come with me.

Peter: Can I bring somebody else?

Jesus: Just bring yourself.

Peter: Will there only be the two of us?

Jesus: Oh no, there'll be plenty of others.

Peter: Will I know some of them?

What about my cousin Alec …
will he be there?

And is there any chance of my sister coming
if she still fancies you?

And what about my gran?
Oh, Jesus, I'd love to bring my gran to meet you.
Can I?

Jesus: Peter … just bring yourself.

Peter: But … but … you said there would be others.

Jesus: That's right.

Peter: Who are they?

Jesus: I'm not telling you.

Peter: Why not?

Jesus: You might not like them.

Peter: Aw, thanks a bunch, Jesus!

(A pause)

Jesus: Peter … ?

Peter: Yes, Jesus???

Jesus: Come with me.

Peter: Jesus, I've got better things to do
than go on a mystery tour.
But I'll think about it.

Just tell me what I'll need.

Jesus: What do you mean?

Peter: Well, if I'm going somewhere I don't know,
with people you refuse to tell me about,
there are some things that might come in very handy.

Jesus: Like what?

Peter: Like something to read in case I get bored …
Like something to sing in case I get sad …

Like a new pair of jeans
in case there's a dance or a party!

Jesus: Peter, you'll not need anything.
Just bring yourself.
That's enough to contend with.

Peter: Jesus ... do you want me to end up like you???

Jesus: Peter ...
I'm going ...

Are you coming with me?

A question of technique

At sunset all who had friends ill with diseases of one kind or another brought them to him; and he laid his hands on them one by one and healed them.

Luke 4: 40

Personnel: **Peter**
Jesus

Peter: Eh ... Jesus ... ?

Jesus: Yes, Peter?

Peter: Can I ask you a question about your technique?

Jesus: What technique, Peter?

Peter: I was afraid you would say that.

Jesus: What's this about?

Peter: It's just that the disciples and I
were trying to work out
what your technique was for healing people.

Jesus: What did you come up with?

Peter: Well, at first we thought it was to do with your hands.

Because when you healed Jairus's daughter
and my old mother-in-law,
you took them by the hand.

But then we remembered the woman
who had been bleeding for twelve years.
You never touched her.

So we decided it wasn't your hands.

Jesus: Well done.
Was there another theory?

Peter: Yes.
Martha thought it was your voice.

Because when you raised Lazarus,
you shouted at him and he came back to life.

But then Andrew reminded us
of how you never saw the centurion's servant,
but you managed to bring him back to life
without shouting at him.

Jesus: So, you decided that it couldn't be my voice.

Peter: That's right.

Oh, Jesus, we even thought
it might be something to do with your saliva.

Jesus: My saliva?

Peter: Well, you did spit on the deaf man's tongue
and that started him yapping
as if it was going out of fashion.

And you spat on mud at the pool of Siloam
and you rubbed the mixture on the blind boy's eyes.

Jesus: But I've healed other deaf people,
and I cured Bartimaeus without spitting.

Peter: Oh, Thomas reminded us of that.

So, the saliva theory is out the window.

Jesus: So, what conclusion did you come to
about my technique?

Peter: Jesus, we don't think you have one!

Jesus: Right fourth time!
I don't have a technique.

Peter: Then how do you heal?

Jesus: Peter,
when Andrew and you were wee (little) boys,
did your mother always treat you the same?

Peter: Oh yes.
She had no favourites.

Jesus: I'm not asking you if she had favourites.
I'm asking you if she treated you the same.

Peter: Well … yes and no.

Jesus: Tell me about the 'no'.

Peter: Let me think …
oh yes, here's an example.

If my mother wanted us to get up in the morning,
she would tell Andrew it was half past seven
and me it was half past eight.

Jesus: Why was that?

Peter: Because she knew
that Andrew loved getting up and I hated it.

The only way she could ever get me out of my bed
was to convince me that I was late.

Jesus: Your mother, Peter,
is like God.

Peter: Don't be daft, Jesus,
my mother wears dentures!

Jesus: Peter, your mother *is* like God.

In order to get you changed
from your pyjamas to your shirt and trousers,
she had to treat you as an individual.

When God, through me,
changes people from being sick to being healthy,
it doesn't happen because of a slick technique.

When you love people,
you treat them and heal them
as individuals.

The big day

John's disciples came to Jesus with the question: 'Why is it that we and the Pharisees fast but your disciples do not?' Jesus replied, 'Can you expect the bridegroom's friends to be sad while he is with them?'

Matthew 9: 14–15

Peter is in a state of great excitement.

Personnel: **Peter**
                 Jesus

Peter: Eh … Jesus … ?

Jesus: Yes, Peter?

Peter: When's the big day, then?

Jesus: Big day?

Peter: You know …
            when do you intend to let the cat out of the bag?

Jesus: I never knew the cat was in the bag.
            In fact, I never knew there was a bag.

Peter: Oh, come on.
            You can tell me …

Jesus: Tell you what?

Peter: Who the lucky lady is …
none of us had any idea.

Jesus: Well, I'd be glad if you would make an informed guess.
For I've no idea either.

Peter: Come on, Jesus, don't muck about.
When are you getting married?

Jesus: Married???

Peter: Jesus, I heard you …
five minutes ago …

You were talking to John's disciples
and you said to them,
'The bridegroom's friends don't fast
while he's with them.'
Didn't you?

Jesus: Yes, but …

Peter: *(Interrupting)*
Then, if you're the bridegroom …
who's the bride?
Where's the wedding?
And who's doing the catering?

Jesus: *Peter …*

Peter: *(Interrupting again)*
Me do the catering?
I'm a lousy cook!

Jesus: Peter …

Peter: Now, Jesus, don't you go all coy.

I heard you.

Jesus: Eh, Peter,
I was speaking metaphorically.

(Pause)

Peter: What do you mean?

Jesus: What you heard was a snippet of a conversation
in which I was trying to explain *your* behaviour.

Peter: *My* behaviour?
What have I done wrong now?

Jesus: Nothing.
You just laugh too much and eat too much
for some people to take you seriously.

Peter: You mean the holy rollers?

Jesus: I think that there are better descriptions
for the Pharisees.

Peter: How about 'whited sepulchres' or 'snakes'?

Jesus: *(Slightly impatiently)*
Peter, the point is that the Pharisees …
and John's disciples …
live a far more moderate life than we do.

They believe that being temperate
and self-controlled is very important.

So, when they see you enjoying a meal
on the day that they decided to fast,
they get a bit upset and a bit judgemental.

Peter: You mean we should be fasting as well?

Jesus: No.
I reminded them that fasting was a voluntary thing.
That's why I said
that when the bridegroom is among his friends
prior to the wedding,
they all enjoy themselves.

Peter: *(Puzzled)*
I don't get it.

Jesus: Well, Peter,
the way I see it is
that the Kingdom of God is like a great feast.

Peter: I know … I remember the story.

Jesus: So, when the sick are cured
or the poor hear the good news or whatever,
that's a sign of the Kingdom coming.
And it's a cause for celebration.

And as I am the one who makes the Kingdom come,
it's only fair that my friends should celebrate with me.

Now do you understand?

Peter: I think so.

(Pause)

Jesus,
if I ask you another question,
will you give me an un-metaphorical answer?

Jesus: What is it?

Peter: When *are* you going to get married?
I mean, you're over thirty
and you're not short of admirers.

Jesus: Peter, there is no answer to that question.

I am here to bring in the Kingdom.
That is what my life is all about.
I couldn't be loyal to my vocation
and to a wife and children.

Peter: But if bringing in the Kingdom is for single people,
why did you choose disciples who are married?

Jesus: Peter, I never said
the work of the Kingdom was for single people.

In my case, it is.
In your case, it's not.

Now, can we go on?

Peter: Just one last question, Jesus …
did you ever fancy Mary Magdalene?

Jesus: Peter … did you ever fancy pork?

Peter: Mum's the word, Jesus.

The sun dances

Look how the wild flowers grow: they do not work or make clothes for themselves. But I tell you that not even King Solomon with all his wealth had clothes as beautiful as one of these flowers. It is God who clothes them ...

Matthew 6: 28–30

Personnel: **Peter**
              Jesus

Peter: Jesus?

Jesus: Yes, Peter?

Peter: Do we have to believe everything
that's written in the Bible?

Jesus: You mean there's something you don't understand?

Peter: *(Surprised)*
How did you know?

Jesus: Intuition, Peter.
Intuition first ... then mind-reading.

Peter: Mind-reading?

Jesus: The passage you are having difficulty with ...
(faking mind-reading)
comes from ...

Psalm ...
65.

Peter: How did you know?
Jesus: Ssshh ...
Psalm 65 ...
verse ...
13.

Peter: Jesus!

Jesus: Ssshh ...
'The valleys are so full of corn,
they laugh and sing.'

Peter: How did you know?

Jesus: *(Oblivious)*
... closely followed by Psalm 148 ...
verse ... 7:
'Praise the Lord from the earth,
you sea monsters and ocean depths.'

Peter: But Jesus ...
how did you know?

(No response)

Go on ... tell us;
are you psychic?

Jesus: No, Peter ... I'm perceptive.
Last week we sang both these psalms in the synagogue.
You were standing two along from me ... remember?

And at these lines you blew a raspberry,
something like ...

(Makes appropriate noise)

Peter: You heard me?

Jesus: Everybody heard you.
There were only six folk at that service.

Peter: Well, no wonder, Jesus.
You can't say these things.

Jesus: What things?

Peter: About valleys laughing
and sea monsters praising God.
It discredits the integrity of the Bible.

Jesus: Peter, in your eyes,
it might discredit the integrity of the Bible.
But in God's eyes,
it expresses the integrity of creation.

Peter: What do you mean?

Jesus: What do I mean?
Answer me this:
what does the thunder do?

Peter: I don't hear any.

Jesus: Then use your memory.
What does the thunder do?

Peter: Roar.

Jesus: What does the wind do?

Peter: Whistle.

Jesus: What does the tide do?

Peter: Comes in and goes out.

Jesus: Proper terms ... ?

Peter: Ebbs and flows?

Jesus: What does the sun do on the waves?

Peter: Dance?

Jesus: What do birds do in the morning?

Peter: Sing.

Jesus: What do flowers do when fully grown?

Peter: Bloom.

Jesus: Who is it all for?

Peter: Pass.

Jesus: No.
No passing.

Who is it all for?
Who is the roaring and the whistling
and the dancing and the singing
– your words, Peter –
who is it all for?

Peter: Us?

Jesus: And what about before 'us' were here, Peter?
Who was it all for then?

Peter: That's a hypothetical question, Jesus!

Jesus: It's nothing of the sort.
You don't need me to tell you
that there was life on earth
before humans walked on two feet.

And there was worship on earth
before humans ever sang a hymn.

Peter: How come?

Jesus: You're just like the rest of them, Peter.
You think that religion
is only for men and women.

You forget
that God made the whole world for his glory.
And that every creature,
in its own way,
is meant to worship him.

That's why the bird sings,
and the tide ebbs and flows,
and the rocks resound,
and the fields get dressed up in bright colours
and the valleys laugh and sing.

Peter: Don't talk romantic, Jesus.

Jesus: I'm not talking romantic.
I'm talking real.

And you and your like-minded friends
had better learn to respect the worship
which earth offers,
because if

– for any reason –
one species of bird no longer sings,
one lake of water no longer sparkles,
one forest of trees no longer claps its hands …
God will want to know why.

Ecology is doxology, Peter.
To care for the earth means to preserve its praise.

Peter: Heavy stuff, Jesus.

Jesus: God's not a lightweight, Peter.

Enjoying yourself

John came, neither eating nor drinking, and people say, 'He is possessed'; the Son of Man came, eating and drinking, and they say, 'Look at him! A glutton and a drinker, a friend of tax-collectors and sinners!'

Matthew 11: 18–19

Personnel: **Peter**
                 Jesus

Peter: Eh, Jesus … ?

Jesus: Yes, Peter?

Peter: Do you always smile when you give people a row?

Jesus: For example, Peter?

Peter: Well, just now …
when you told off the Pharisees
for complaining that we enjoyed ourselves.

You were grinning all over your face
and they were getting more and more livid.

Jesus: Well, that's their problem.
If only they read the bits of the Bible
which they strenuously avoid,
they would see that God's people
have always enjoyed themselves.

Peter: Have they?

Jesus: I think we should have a little quiz, Peter.

Peter: Who's asking the questions?

Jesus: I am.
You can answer them.

Number one:
what did Sarah do
when she heard that she was to become pregnant?

Peter: Tell her mother?

Jesus: Wrong.
Her mother had been dead for fifty years.
She giggled.

Peter: Giggled?

Jesus: Number two:
what did Joseph do
when he was reunited with his brothers
who had sold him into slavery?

Peter: Cut off their hands!

Jesus: He threw a party.

Peter: A party?

Jesus: Number three:
what did Miriam do
when she had crossed through the Red Sea?

Peter: Dry her hair?

Jesus: Danced.

Peter: Danced?

Jesus: Number four:
what are Harvest, New Year and Shelters?

Peter: Festivals!

Jesus: Well done!
Number five:
what did Saul do when he was anointed king?

Peter: Get a new suit?

Jesus: No, he began to dance.

Peter: Dance?

Jesus: Number six:
what did David do
which disgusted his wife?

Peter: He argued with her old man?

Jesus: No.
He danced in public.

Peter: Danced?

Jesus: Number seven:
what are the trees of the field meant to do?

Peter: ... Dance?

Jesus: No.
Clap their hands.

Number eight:
what are the mountains meant to do?

Peter: … Clap their hands as well?

Jesus: No. Skip like rams.

Peter: Skip like rams?

Jesus: Yes … and the hills are meant to skip like lambs.

Enjoying this, Peter?

Number nine.

Peter: I hope this is an easy one …

Jesus: Of course it is.
Name five parties we've been at.

Peter: Simon's house.

Jesus: Mm-hm …

Peter: The rich Pharisee's house.

Jesus: Mm-hm …

Peter: Matthew's house …
and Zaccheus's house.

Jesus: Mm-hm …

Peter: Martha and Mary's house.

Jesus: No, that was just afternoon tea.

Peter: Where else?

Jesus: Your house!

Peter: My house?

Jesus: Yes, after I healed your mother-in-law.

Peter: Oh, I forgot.

Jesus: Well, I certainly haven't forgotten you
running about like a bear with a sore paw, saying,
'Jesus, have you any idea
how much this is costing me?'

Peter: Did I?

Jesus: It doesn't matter.

What does matter is that God has intended
that people enjoy themselves on earth ...
and also that the earth enjoys itself ...
that's why there's all that talk
about trees clapping their hands.

Peter: But is it right to enjoy yourself
when people are starving
or are poor
or are being treated like scum?

Jesus: Well, it doesn't help if you go on a guilt trip.

What does matter
is that your enjoyment
shouldn't cost other people their health
or their happiness.

There's enough for everybody
if everybody lives wisely.

Peter: I see ...
well, what's next.

Jesus: One more question, Peter.
Number ten:
what are the Pharisees currently calling me?

Peter: Do you really want to know?

Jesus: Answer the question, Peter.

Peter: They're making out
that you're a drunkard and a glutton.

(Pause)

Jesus: So ... what's next?

Peter: What do you mean?

Jesus: Well, should *I* go on a diet
of locusts and wild honey
or should *we* go to Martha and Mary's
for some home-made chocolate eclairs?

Peter: I'll lead the way, Jesus.

Contamination

A Pharisee invited Jesus to a meal; he went to the house and took his place at table. A woman who was living an immoral life in the town had learned that Jesus was a guest in the Pharisee's house and had brought oil of myrrh in a small flask.

Luke 7: 36–37

Personnel: **Peter**
Jesus

Peter: Jesus ... ?

Jesus: Yes, Peter?

Peter: Are you never afraid you'll get contaminated?

Jesus: Not as long as you wash your hands
between cleaning the hen run
and mixing the salad dressing.

Peter: Not from food ...
from people.

Jesus: Oh, you mean the wee girl with the measles?

Peter: No, not children ... adults ... like *that* woman.

Jesus: Which woman?

Peter: You know the one.

Jesus: You mean Rebecca.

Peter: That's not what most folk call her.

Jesus: Maybe not, but I'm not most folk.

Peter: Jesus, she's a wee hoor (slut).

Jesus: I think there might be a better description.

Peter: Okay … well, she's a tart.

Jesus: Well, that's your opinion, Peter.

Peter: Jesus, she had the hots for you.
She was all over you.

And you just sat there
while she cried all over your feet.

It was a liberty.
And you never did a thing.
You want to hear what people are saying.

Jesus: I can imagine.
I hear what you're saying.

Peter: So …

Jesus: So … ?

Peter: Jesus, you don't know where she's been.
She's probably riddled with the pox
and she'll have crabs.

Jesus: You seem to be quite an expert
on women's diseases, Peter.

Peter: Come off it, Jesus.
You're not making a fool of me.
You're making a fool of yourself.

Jesus: *(Sternly)*
So, what if I am?
What is it to you, Peter?
Are you worried about your reputation?

Just remember that when I first met you,
you were no blue-eyed boy.
You swore like a trooper and you stank of fish
and you were as sensitive as a tickling stick at a funeral.

Peter: But I wasn't a hoor (slut).

Jesus: No, you were worse than a hoor (slut).
At least Rebecca knows she's done wrong.
You thought you were the bee's knees.

People don't contaminate me,
because, unlike you,
I don't go looking for the dirt in them,
I go looking for the gold.

Plenty of people tell Rebecca she's a slut.

Plenty of people used to shout 'unclean' at Joel
because he was a leper and had fingers missing.

Plenty of people still whisper behind Matthew's back
that he used to be a con merchant (racketeer).

There's dirt in everybody.
But those who know how bad they've been
don't need you or me to remind them
or to stand back in case we get contaminated.

When you look at Rebecca, you see a whore;
when I look at her, I see an apprentice angel …
and it's the same with Joel …
and it's the same with Matthew.

Peter: But what about your reputation?

Jesus: Peter,
what about their lives?

Going under

Peter called to him: 'Lord, if it is you, tell me to come to you over the water.' 'Come,' said Jesus. Peter got out of the boat and walked over the water towards Jesus. But when he saw the strength of the gale, he was afraid; and beginning to sink, he cried, 'Save me, Lord!'

Matthew 14: 28–30

Peter is evidently embarrassed.

Personnel: **Jesus**
                 Peter

Jesus: Peter ... ?

Peter: *(No response)*

Jesus: Peter ... ?

Peter: *(No response)*

Jesus: Is it as bad as that?

Peter: Mm-hm.

Jesus: But you've changed your clothes ...
            you're dry now.

Peter: It wasn't getting wet that bothered me.
            It was making such a fool of myself.

Why did you let me do it?
Surely you knew what would happen?

Jesus: What have the others said?

Peter: They've been quite good actually,
apart from Andrew
who keeps making snide comments about webbed feet.

Jesus: Well, your shoulders are broad enough.

Peter: It's not my feet or my shoulders, Jesus,
it's my head.
Whatever made me try it?

Jesus: Well, you tell me ...
Why did you try it?

Peter: Oh, you know what I'm like.
I take these daft notions ...
I always want to be in on the act
and you made it look so easy.

We all thought it was a ghost at first.
I mean, treading grapes is one thing,
but walking on water is out of the question.

Then we realised it wasn't a ghost.
It was you ...
and you *were* walking on the sea.

Jesus: And you wanted to do the same ... eh?

Peter: Yes, I did.

Jesus: Why, Peter?

Peter: A bit of me wanted to see if I could do it ...

Jesus: And a bit of you wanted to show off ... eh?

Peter: Yes ... yes, that's right.
But I did manage it at first, didn't I?

Jesus: Yes you did ...
for about five yards.
And then ... ?

Peter: After that I don't remember a thing
until I woke up in the boat
with James pulling seaweed out of my mouth.

What happened?

Jesus: I'll tell you what happened.
You stopped looking at me
and started looking at the waves.

Peter: I could hardly do anything else.
There was a big swell.

Jesus: Remember Lot's wife, Peter.

Peter: Did she try walking on water?

Jesus: No ... but like you, instead of looking ahead,
she began to get fascinated
by the danger all around her ...
and she ended up being destroyed.

Peter: I'm not sure of what you're saying.

Jesus: Peter, I've asked you to follow me.
And you can only follow me

if you watch what I'm doing
and see where I'm going.

And wherever I am,
there will be trouble and opposition.
There will be threats all around you
and there will be distractions inside you ...
doubt ...
uncertainty ...
and all the old temptations
you thought you'd left behind.

If you keep your eye on these things,
you'll go under.

If you keep your eye on me,
you'll stay afloat.

Peter: Is it as easy as that?

Jesus: No, Peter.
It's not as easy as that.
It's not easy at all.

Peter: Do you ever feel like giving up on me, Jesus?

Jesus: No.

Peter: *(After a moment)*
... Anything else?

Jesus: Yes ...
it's high time you learnt how to swim.

Of mouths and money

No slave can serve two masters; for either he will hate the first and love the second, or he will be devoted to the first and despise the second. You cannot serve God and Money.

Luke 16: 13

Personnel: **Jesus**
Peter

Jesus: Eh ... Peter?

Peter: Yes, Jesus?

Jesus: Did I interrupt a wee (little) gambling session earlier on?

Peter: What makes you think that?

Jesus: Well, sound travels in the open air,
and as I came down from the hills
I heard voices raised in a rather unusual fashion.

Peter: What did you hear?

Jesus: I heard John shouting,
'I bet you it's sex!'

Then I heard Andrew shouting,
'I bet you it's hell!'

Then I heard Judas shouting,

'Put your money where your mouth is!'

And then I heard you.

Peter: And what did I say?

Jesus: 'Sshh … Jesus is coming.'

And then it all went quiet.
Now, were you gambling or … ?

Peter: Oh, nothing like that, Jesus.
We were just having a minor disagreement.

Jesus: A minor disagreement about what?

Peter: About you … or about what you say.
It was stupid in a way.

We were arguing about which subject
you talked about the most.

Jesus: I see.
What was on your short list?

Peter: We thought that it was either …
personal morality,
family life,
hell,
domestic economics or …

Jesus: (*Interrupting*)
Hold on.
One at a time.
What were they again?

Peter: Personal morality.

Jesus: You mean sex?

Peter: Well, yes …
but that was John's idea, remember.

Jesus: And the others?

Peter: Hell …

Jesus: Mm-hm …

Peter: Family life …

Jesus: Mm-hm …

Peter: Domestic economics …

Jesus: You mean money?

Peter: Yes …
and there was another one …
the 'eschatological issue' …

Jesus: The what?

Peter: Oh, Jesus, don't ask me to say it again.
I heard it from a rabbi.
It means the end of time, the last judgement, the …

Jesus: It's all right, Peter, I know what it means.
And I'm pleased to know that you understand it.

But in future, don't try to sound like a priest.
Stick to layperson's language … like me.

Peter: Sorry, Jesus.

Jesus: So, which one did you decide on?

Peter: We never made a decision ...
you interrupted the conversation.

Jesus: Well, which one do you think I talk about most?

Peter: I know it's not sex or hell.
And I don't think it's family life.

Jesus: What about the 'eschatological issue'?

Peter: No, I don't think so.

I reckon it must be money.

Jesus: What brings you to that conclusion?

Peter: It's just when I think about your stories,
I reckon that you've told more parables about money
than about anything else.
I can remember at least half a dozen.

Jesus: Half a dozen?

Peter: Well, there's the Treasure in the Field,
The Talents,
The Rich Fool ... eh ...
The Great Feast ...
Dives and Lazarus ... and ...
The Lost Coin.

Jesus: Well done.

Come to think of it, there are probably another six,
but I haven't told you them all yet.

Peter: Jesus, are you obsessed with money?

Jesus: No. I'm not obsessed with money.
And in any case, Peter,
my parables are not about economics,
domestic or otherwise.

They are about the Kingdom ...
about forgiveness, justice, love.

Peter: But Jesus,
you do talk a lot about money.

I mean,
think of what you said to the rich young man ...
and the conversation about the widow's mite ...
and all your talk
about not being able to serve God and wealth.

You say more about money than you do about prayer!

Jesus: That may be right, Peter.
And if it is,
it's because people would rather hear me talking
about spiritual things than about material things.

They'd rather hear a sermon about their souls
than a sermon about their shares.

Peter: So do you do it to annoy them?

Jesus: No, Peter.

It's just that more and more I realise
that behind a lot of spiritual blindness,
and behind a lot of injustice in the world,
there's a money problem.

And where that's the case,
then it's safer to talk about faith than about finances.
But God's interested in both.

Peter: You should have been a businessman, Jesus.

Jesus: Oh no, Peter ...
that's not my calling.

As regards money, my vocation is not to have any.

In that way I can get close to poor folk
and let the rich know
that all their piety and religion doesn't count ...
until they put their money where God's mouth is.

Peter: Where 'God's mouth' is?

Jesus: Think about it, Peter.

Now, come on.
I've got other things to discuss with you.

Peter: Like what?

Jesus: Well, we could start with the 'eschatological issue' ...

S.O.S.

For while some are incapable of marriage because they were born so, or were made so by men, there are others who have renounced marriage for the sake of the Kingdom of Heaven. Let those accept who can.

Matthew 19:12

Personnel: **Peter**
              Jesus

Peter: Eh … Jesus … ?

Jesus: Yes, Peter?

Peter: You never talk about sex.

Jesus: Why do you say that, Peter, do you have a problem?

Peter: No.

Jesus: Well, what's bothering you?

Peter: You never talk about sex.

Jesus: Peter, you do have a problem!

Peter: No, I don't.

Jesus: Then what do you expect me to say?

I mean,
you're a married man.
You've got three children.
It seems to me
that the birds and bees are in working order.

Peter: It's not to do with me.

Jesus: Oh … so somebody else has a problem.
Name names, Peter.

Is it your brother, Andrew?
I thought I saw him
giving Mary Magdalene the glad eye the other day.

Peter: No.
It's just that you never talk about the subject.

Jesus: So … ?
I don't talk about the exchange rate
or Greek poetry
or archaeological digs near the Red Sea
but I never hear you complaining.

Peter: Jesus, you're avoiding the issue!

Jesus: Maybe I am, Peter.

Peter: But why?

Jesus: Maybe it's because I'm not an expert in everything.

Maybe it's because I'm a single man
and intend to remain that way.

Maybe it's because there are some things
you'd like to hear me saying,

but you don't write my script, Peter.

God does.
And there are other things God wants me to say.

Peter: But what have we to tell young people?
What have we to tell folk
who've got a problem about sex?

Jesus: Okay, Peter ...
Tell them three things.

Tell them that sex, unlike food,
is not compulsory.
It's important for you ...
but it's not important for me,
though I'm every bit as much a man as you are.

Secondly,
tell them to love themselves.

Because if they can't love themselves,
then they shouldn't encourage anybody else
to do it for them.

And thirdly,
tell them to read the Bible.

Peter: The Bible ...
but it condemns it.
It just makes you feel guilty.

Jesus: Peter, the Bible does not condemn sex.
It condemns abusing people,
using people,
and it condemns turning a gift of God
into an object of cheap pleasure.

But the Bible also says
some very positive things about love
– physical love, even.

Peter: It does?

Jesus: It does.

Peter: Where?

Jesus: *(Quietly)*
S.O.S.

Peter: S.O.S.?
(Louder)
S.O.S.???

Jesus: Sshh, Peter …

Song of Solomon …

Don't tell everybody …
It might become a best seller!

A new experience

And I say to you: you are Peter, the Rock; and on this rock I will build my church and the powers of death shall never conquer it. I will give you the keys of the Kingdom of Heaven; what you forbid on earth shall be forbidden in Heaven, and what you allow on earth shall be allowed in Heaven.

Matthew 16: 18–19

Personnel: **Peter**
Jesus

Peter: Eh ... Jesus ... ?

Jesus: Yes, Peter ... ?

Peter: Eh ... I was just thinking ...

Jesus: Is that a new experience, Peter?

Peter: I was just thinking about this ... eh ... church.

Jesus: Which church, Peter?

Peter: The one ... the one you're going to build ... on me.

Jesus: Oh, that church.
Well, what were you thinking?

Peter: Eh ... I was thinking
that I'm not exactly the world's best administrator.

Jesus: There are some people who would say
that you weren't exactly the world's best fisherman.

Peter: Oh, Jesus … you said you wouldn't mention that again!

Jesus: Sorry, Peter.
Now … you were saying …

Peter: I was saying that I'm not the world's best administrator
and you haven't exactly given me much of a clue
as to what I should do.

Jesus: What do you mean?

Peter: Well, for example …
who is the church for?

Is it just for the Jews?

Jesus: No.

Peter: Is it just for Gentiles?

Jesus: No.

Peter: Is it for everybody?

Jesus: Mm-hm.

Peter: Including women???

Jesus: Mm-hm.

Peter: Jesus!!!

Jesus: Yes, Peter … ?

Peter: Do you know what you're letting yourself in for?
I mean, do you know what you're letting *me* in for?

Jesus: Do you have something against women?

Peter: No, I'm married to one.
But, I mean, in the synagogue they know their place.

Jesus: I thought we were talking about the church.

Peter: Exactly!
If they don't know their place in the church,
they'll ruin everything.

Jesus: You mean they might get things organised?

Peter: Well ... yes ...

Jesus: And that would be a new experience ...
wouldn't it?

Peter: Well ... well ...
Look, quite apart from the women,
what do you want the men to do?

Do you want us to sing ...
standing up or sitting down?

Do you want us to kneel to pray,
or stretch our hands in the air?

Do you want candles and incense ...
or has the church to be a smokeless zone?

Are there to be speakers or silence?

Do you want drums and trumpets?

I mean, Thomas suggested guitars,
but I told him that guitars gave God a sore head.

Jesus: What gave you that impression?

Peter: Amos 5, verse 23 ... remember?

Jesus: Oh ... of course ...

Peter: And another thing, Jesus ...
how do you want it run?

Jesus: Run?

Peter: Yes ... how do you want it run?

James says it should be a territorial democracy.
Andrew thought it might be a centralised bureaucracy.
Simon said that people should do as they please ...
but he's just an anarchist!

What do you say?

Jesus: Not very much.

Peter: Jesus, be serious.

I mean ...
you said that you were going to build the church on me,
but you don't give me a clue
as to what it should be like.

What happens if you disappear and I drop dead?
Will the whole thing go up in a puff of smoke?

Jesus: Well, that would be an interesting way
of finding your successor.

Peter: Pardon?

Jesus: Peter, Peter, don't worry about the church.
That's God's problem, not yours.
You set your eyes on the kingdom
and God will make clear
what should be the shape of the church.

For God wants the church
to be the servant of the kingdom,
not the master;
to celebrate the kingdom,
not to dominate it;
to be a sign of the good news,
not just a reminder of the bad.

(Pause)

Peter: Jesus ...
I don't think you've answered any of my questions.

Jesus: Is that a new experience, Peter?

Peter: No, Jesus.

The silver coin

Go and cast a line in the lake; take the first fish you catch, open its mouth and you will find a silver coin; take that and pay the tax for us both.

Matthew 17: 27

Peter is distracted; Jesus is nonchalant.

Personnel: **Peter**
Jesus

Peter: Eh … Jesus … ?

Jesus: Yes, Peter … ?

Peter: Eh … I've got …
eh … we've got …
eh … I think there's a problem!

Jesus: Yes, Peter?

Peter: It's a problem about money.

Jesus: I see … so, what's the problem?

Peter: Eh … we don't have any.

Jesus: But that's nothing new, Peter.

Peter: No, Jesus.

(A pause)

Peter: Eh … Jesus?

Jesus: Yes, Peter?

Peter: What do you think about taxes?

Jesus: I've never been in one, Peter.

Peter: No … not taxis … *taxes!*

Jesus: Well, what do you think about them?

Peter: I worry when we don't have money to pay them.

That's the problem …
we're going to Capernaum …
when we get there,
they'll ask us to pay taxes.

And that means money …
and … and we don't have any.

Jesus: But that's nothing new, Peter.

Peter: No, Jesus.

(A pause)

Peter: Eh … Jesus?

Jesus: *(Getting exasperated)*
Yes, Peter!!

Peter: What are you going to do then?

Jesus: What am I going to do then?

You mean, what are *you* going to do then!

Peter: Yes ... I mean, what are you going to do then ... ?
I mean ... what am *I* going to do then?

Jesus: You're going to stop worrying ...
and start fishing.

Peter: Fishing???

Jesus: That's right.

You're going to take a line and throw it in the lake.
And when you pull it out,
you'll find you've caught a big fish ...
with a silver coin in its mouth.

Peter: Jesus, I've heard of gold fillings ...
but this is ridiculous!

How could a fish have a silver coin in its mouth?

Jesus: Oh, it'll get one ...
when you take it to the market ...

It's amazing how much some folk will give
for a five-pound salmon.

Peter: *(Slowly realising)*
Oh, I see.

Jesus: Had you not thought of that?

Peter: No, Jesus, I didn't think.

Jesus: But that's nothing new, Peter.

Peter: No, Jesus.

A simple question

The disciples came to Jesus and asked, 'Who is the greatest in the Kingdom of Heaven?' He called a child, set him in front of them and said, 'Truly I tell you: unless you turn round and become like children, you will never enter the Kingdom of Heaven.'

Matthew 18: 1–3

Personnel: **Peter**
Jesus

Peter: Eh ... Jesus ... ?

Jesus: Yes, Peter ... ?

Peter: Eh ... can I ask you a simple question?

Jesus: As long as you don't expect a simple answer.

Peter: Eh ... well,
it's about a certain statement you made the other day,
much to the displeasure of certain people.

Jesus: Would these 'certain people'
wander about the Galilean countryside
with only a stick and one set of clothing?

Peter: Eh ... perhaps ...

Jesus: So, I've upset the disciples again ... eh?

Peter: Well … I'm not one for gossip.

Jesus: All right, what did I say?

Peter: You said we've to become like children!

Jesus: You were listening, Peter …

Peter: More than that,
you said we wouldn't get into the Kingdom
unless we became like little children.

Jesus: So?

Peter: So … what did you mean?

Jesus: Well, Peter, how would you describe children?

Peter: (*Slowly*)
Naive …
innocent …
harmless, I suppose …
oh, and a bit wet sometimes!

Jesus: … innocent, harmless, wet …
Peter, how many kids do you have?

Peter: Jesus, thanks to you
I've hardly seen my wife for three years.
But at the last count, we didn't have any.

Jesus: Then the quicker you have some, the better.
You'll soon find out
that they're not innocent, naive or harmless.

Anyone who thinks differently
has never been in a nursery.

Peter: So, what are they like?

Jesus: Use your memory, Peter.
Think of the children we've met.

Peter: We haven't met any.

Jesus: What about the ones in the temple ... ?

Peter: Jesus, they sounded like the cats' choir
and you had the cheek to say
they were 'perfecting God's praise'.

Jesus: Peter,
our musical tastes may differ,
but I don't think you can deny
that they were really enthusiastic.

Peter: Not like the Pharisees ... eh, Jesus?

Jesus: Not like the Pharisees
and not like a lot of adults
who think that God's only pleased
when you look as delirious as an undertaker's dummy.

Peter: So, we've to be enthusiastic.
Anything else?

Jesus: Think of a girl, Peter ...
Jairus's daughter.

What do you remember of her?

Peter: Now if ever there was an undertaker's dummy ...

Jesus: That's right.
But she trusted me.

I said 'get up' and she got up.

How many adults take me at my word ...
including a certain company
of ex-civil servants and fishermen?

Peter: So, we've to be enthusiastic and trustful.
Is that it?

Jesus: There's more, Peter.

Think of a field ...
Five thousand people ...
what shall we give them to eat ... ?

Peter: Oh, you mean the wee boy I brought to you.

Jesus: Peter, where is your memory?
Andrew brought the wee (little) boy.
You just stood and giggled.

But what quality did the wee (little) boy show?
... it begins with a 'g'...

Peter: Eh ... generosity.

Jesus: Peter, you should try crosswords.

Peter: So, to be like children
we should be enthusiastic, trustful and generous.

Jesus: There's something else.

Peter: There always is!

Jesus: Do you remember the crowd of men
who surrounded me,

wanting to ask me very cultured questions ...
do you remember who came through the crowd?

Peter: You don't mean the wee lassie (little girl)
with jam on her face?

Jesus: I most certainly do.

Peter: Do we have to get jam on our face
to get into the Kingdom of Heaven?

Jesus: No.
But think of what her mother said
when she came to take her back.
She was all apologetic.

She said,
'I'm sorry, mister, she's awful curious.'

Peter: So, is curiosity one of the things
we should learn from children?

Jesus: Yes ...
and in that department, Peter,
you get ten out of ten.

F.T. index

Hearing that Jesus had silenced the Sadducees, the Pharisees came together in a body, and one of them tried to catch him out with a question.

Matthew 22: 34–35

Personnel: **Peter**
Jesus

Peter: Eh … Jesus?

Jesus: Yes, Peter?

Peter: I've just been looking at the crowd.

Jesus: Aha … and … ?

Peter: … and there's a lot of F.T.s about today.

Jesus: What's an F.T., Peter?
I was never very good at acronyms.

Peter: Pharisee Types.

Jesus: *(Pause)*
Pharisee Types?

Peter: Uh huh.
I've counted at least twenty-nine.

Jesus: It's not your arithmetic I want to dispute, Peter ...
it's your spelling.

Pharisee is spelt with a P, not an F.

Peter: Make allowances, Jesus.
I'm just an illiterate fisherman ... remember?

Jesus: Well, that's your story.

But tell me,
why are you worried about the Pharisees?

Peter: Because they're on the increase ...
I mean, when we started with you,
we never saw them,
except when we went into a synagogue or the Temple.
And they certainly never came looking for us.
You were beneath their contempt,
but now it's a different story.

Jesus: Peter, to some extent that has to be expected.
Wherever there is the possibility of good,
there's also the potential for evil.

The more we ...
and I mean all of us ...
preach or teach or heal
we have to expect criticism and confrontation.

The Gospel is a threat to the status quo,
not its sanctifier.

Peter: But, Jesus,
there are more and more of them,
and they've got influence ...
influential friends in high places

and dicey friends in low places.
And they've got power.

Jesus: And you haven't?

Peter: Jesus ...
my name used to be Simon ...
not Samson.

Jesus: Let me tell you, Peter ...
if you were a candle ...
just a wee (tiny) light ...
all the darkness in the world couldn't put you out.
And you, small as you were,
would have more power than all the darkness.

Peter: *(Impatiently)*
Yes, Jesus ...
but I'm not a candle.

Jesus: Yes, I know that.
But if you are, as you say,
an illiterate fisherman,
and my Spirit lives in you,
then you will be more powerful
than all the Pharisees and their lackeys put together.

Peter: Well, I'm not so sure about that.

Jesus: Well, be sure about this:
that the people to fear
– if you must fear the powerful –
are not those who look threatening
and would harm you.

Fear, rather, those who seem friendly
but who do nothing.

The biggest threat to the Gospel
is not those who are obviously bad
but those who are apathetic.

Peter: Well, Jesus,
I know how to spot the Pharisee Types,
but how do you spot the apathetics?

Jesus: I'm not telling you.

Peter: Why not?

Jesus: Because your job
is not just to be on the defence against evil
but to be on the attack with the good.

Peter: Jesus ...
that's very military language.

Jesus: Sorry, Peter ...
it must be seeing the centurions in the crowd.

Peter: Are you sure they're centurions?

Jesus: Why, what do you think they are?

Peter: F.T.s in fancy dress ...

In God's image

And here is this woman, a daughter of Abraham, who has been bound by Satan for eighteen long years: was it not right for her to be loosed from her bonds on the Sabbath?

Luke 13:16

Personnel: **Peter**
Jesus

Peter: Eh ... Jesus ... ?

Jesus: Yes, Peter?

Peter: Do you know how it says in the Bible
that God made man and woman in his own image?

Jesus: Yes.

Peter: Is that true?

Jesus: Yes ... why?

Peter: Well ...
men and women are ...
not the same ...
they're ... you know ...
different.

Jesus: Is this a gender awareness lesson, Peter?

Peter: No ... I just can't understand
how men and women can be like God
if they're not like each other.

Jesus: But, Peter, you look very like your sisters.

I've seen them ...
they have the same kind of hair as you,
they have the same black eyes,
they have the same small nose.

Peter: Yes ... but not all parts are the same.

Jesus: I'm quite aware of that.

Peter: Jesus, but never mind men and women.
Not all men are the same.

Some men are very tall, some are fat.
Some have a lot of hair, some are bald.
Some have black skins, some have white skins.

Jesus: *(Mimicking)*
Some never speak, some never shut up.

Peter: *(A little taken aback)*
Yes ...
are they all made in God's image?

Jesus: Yes.

Peter: What about a blind man
with only one leg?
Is he made in God's image?

Jesus: Yes.

Peter: What about a woman
with no teeth and big ears?
Is she made in God's image?

Jesus: Yes.

Peter: What about a baby dying of hunger?
Is it made in God's image?

Jesus: Yes.

Peter: What about ... ?

Jesus: *(Interrupting)*
Peter, Peter, that's enough.

Peter: But I'm just trying to point out
that everybody is different.
There are no two people the same.

Jesus: Exactly.
That's what it means to he made in God's image.

There is only one God.
God is unique.
And the people who God makes are all,
like him,
unique.

Peter: But what about the people who are evil?
What about the people who abuse children,
or terrorists who kill innocent civilians?

Surely they're not made in God's image?

Jesus: Yes, they are.

Peter: But, Jesus!

Jesus: But, Peter …
to be unique is not the same as to be good.

God makes us all unique and he loves us all uniquely.
But whether we are good or bad is up to us.

Peter: But what about the starving child?

Jesus: The starving child is also made in God's image.
The starving child is also unique.

And perhaps only when people appreciate
the value of each individual life,
there will be no more starving children …
for all will be fed;
and perhaps no more criminals,
because they will have been loved.

Peter: Do you never wish
that people weren't so different?
Would it not be easier if some were the same?

Jesus: Do you mean, would I like two of you?

Peter: Well, perhaps, Jesus.

Jesus: Definitely not, Peter.

Sophistication

Today salvation has come to this house – for this man too is a son of Abraham. The Son of Man has come to seek and to save the lost.

Luke 19: 9–10

Personnel: **Peter**
Jesus

Peter: Eh … Jesus?

Jesus: Yes, Peter?

Peter: How come …
how come you're not very sophisticated?

Jesus: Sophisticated?

Peter: Aye (yes) … sophisticated.

Jesus: Is it the way I dress, Peter?
Do you think I'd look better in a college scarf?

Peter: No, I don't mean the way you dress.

Jesus: Well, is it what I eat?

I saw you turning up your nose
at the camel-cheese quiche
we were offered the other day.

Peter: No, it's not what you eat …
though I must say, Jesus,
you have a shock-proof stomach.

Jesus: Well, is it my hairstyle?
… my table manners?
… my singing voice?

Peter: Jesus, this is just like you.
I ask a question and you turn it into a conundrum.

I'm talking about your language.

Jesus: Peter,
are you by any chance going to complain
because I don't …
magniverbalise?

Peter: *(Confused)*
Because you don't *magniverbalise?*

Jesus: Because I don't use big words?

Peter: Yes … but how do you know that?

Jesus: Oh, just a hunch.

Peter: You see, people expect
that if you are the 'S.O.G.' …

Jesus: *(Interrupting)*
Pardon???

Peter: The Son of God …
you should be a bit more …
you know …
intellectual.

Jesus: Peter, this is quite irrelevant.

Peter: Jesus,
don't avoid the issue.
You know what I mean.

You never say words like Pentateuch.
You never talk about yourself as the Messiah
or the Redeemer.
You never mention salvation.

Jesus: Never?

Peter: Okay, you did once.

Jesus: And do you remember the occasion?

Peter: Yes …
it was the day you went to Zaccheus's house.

Jesus: And do you remember when I used the word?

Peter: Yes, I do …
because it took me by surprise.

You had invited yourself back to his house.
You had eaten a meal with him;
you had heard him say
that he wanted to follow you;
you watched him giving away his money
to the folk he had swindled;
then you said a prayer and gave him a big hug.

And just as you put your foot out of the door,
you said, 'Salvation has come to this house.'

Jesus: That's exactly right, Peter.

And do you know why I said it?

Because Zaccheus had had an experience ...
and I put a name on it.

That's the way it is with me.

If I start with religious jargon
before I know people's names,
I set up a barrier between them and me.

But once I've learned their names
and shared their food
and talked of heaven in their language,
then I might become what you might call 'sophisticated'.

Peter: But Jesus,
do you never worry about your credibility?

Jesus: Never, Peter,
and neither should you.

The Gospel is *not* credible.
It is incredible.

I want people to be amazed by God's love,
not mesmerised by my language.

Set apart

You did not choose me: I chose you. I appointed you to go on and bear fruit, fruit that will last.

John 15:16

Personnel: **Peter**
Jesus

Peter: Eh ... Jesus ... ?

Jesus: Yes, Peter ... ?

Peter: Do you mind if I ask you a personal question?

Jesus: I haven't got a penny on me, Peter.

Peter: No, it's not about money.

Jesus: Then what is it about?

Peter: It's just ...
eh ... it's just ...
eh ... are you ...
you know ... 'ordained'?

Jesus: Am I ... you know ... 'ordained'?
What do you mean?

Peter: Well, have you had hands laid on you?

Jesus: My mother used to clip my ear when I was a boy.
Does that count?

Peter: No! ...
I mean have you been 'set apart'?

Jesus: Oh, regularly.
The Pharisees do it every time I go near them.

Peter: Jesus, do you know what I'm talking about?

Jesus: Yes.

Yes, I do know what you're talking about.
But why are you asking me the question?

Peter: Just because everybody who's special in God's eyes
seems to have been ordained.

Jesus: Like who?

Peter: Well ... like Abraham, I suppose.

Jesus: Eh ... Peter ... Abraham wasn't ordained.
He just stopped enjoying his retirement
and started travelling.

Peter: What about his wife?

Jesus: You mean Sarah?
She became pregnant.
That's not the same as becoming ordained.

Peter: What about David?
Did he not get ordained?

Jesus: No, he got crowned.

And that's not the same.

Peter: … just like getting pregnant.

Jesus: No.
A pregnancy and a coronation are entirely different.

Peter: Jesus, I know that.
My mother had four children.
She'd rather have had a coronation any day.

Jesus: Never mind your mother.
Who else do you think was ordained?

Peter: Eh … Daniel.

Jesus: No.
He was a diplomat
who was good with dangerous animals.

Peter: What about Amos?

Jesus: No.
He was a shepherd who was good with words.

Peter: Well, Jeremiah then.

Jesus: No.
He was an eccentric who was good for an argument.

Peter: Jesus, surely some famous folk got ordained?

Jesus: Oh yes.
Some did.
There have always been priests ordained and set apart
to attend to the mysteries of the faith.

But there also have been prophets and pioneers,
many unordained,
whose job it has been to demonstrate the will of God
in places where the priests made no impact.

Peter: So, is it important to be ordained?

Jesus: Peter, the day will come when,
because you are neither a priest nor a prophet,
you will be sneered at.

People will look at you and the others who follow me.
And they'll ridicule you for being 'untrained laypeople'.
You will then wish you were a priest or prophet,
set apart and able to hide behind your special office.

But what really matters
is not to be known as special
but to be seen as faithful
to the one who has chosen you.

(Pause)

Peter: So you don't want me to become a rabbi
or a father or a reverend?

Jesus: Peter, I want you to be my disciple.

Anything else is second place.
Anything less is second best.

The protector

The light will be among you a little longer. Continue on your way while you have the light, so that the darkness will not come upon you; for the one who walks in the dark does not know where he is going. Believe in the light then, while you have it, so that you will be the people of the light.

John 12: 35–36

Peter is in a sullen, angry mood.

Personnel: **Jesus**
Peter

Jesus: Peter?

Peter: Yes, Jesus?

Jesus: What's up?

Peter: Nothing.

Jesus: Peter, you look like an advert for the toothache, and you have done all day.
Now, what's up?

Peter: Nothing.

Jesus: Nothing always smiles …
something always frowns.

Peter: What?

Jesus: 'Nothing always smiles ...
something always frowns'
– it's just a saying of my mother's.
Oh, come on.
Tell me what's bugging you.

Peter: Never mind.

Jesus: Peter, what's bugging you?

Peter: *(In an outburst)*
You!!!

You're bugging me!

Honestly, you tell us to follow you
and so we do.
And we end up seeing the back of your neck
more than anything else.

And you're always moving.
It's always the next town,
the next crowd,
the next cripple.

And we're always tagging on behind, feeling lousy.

And people, of course,
expect us to do the things you do.
But you don't have to cope with them
when they find we can't.

Jesus: *(Quietly)*
Faith and prayer, Peter.
Faith and prayer ...

Peter: Don't 'faith and prayer' me, Jesus.
I've had enough.

When did you last take us for a drink
or ask us how we feel?

And what about when you go?
What will happen then?

Do you ever think of the 'great legacy'
you're leaving us?

(Pause)

Jesus: What do you feel about me ...
just now ...
Peter?

Peter: I feel as if I hate you.

Jesus: And how do you feel about yourself?

Peter: Despair ... I just despair.

Jesus: And why have you never said this before?

(Silence)

Why, Peter?

Peter: *(More calmly)*
Because I never thought I could say it.
I never thought you could take it.

Jesus: Peter, Peter ...
if I wanted to be protected,
I would have stayed in heaven.

Peter: Pardon?

Jesus: Peter,
I came to earth to meet my people
and to let them know that they could meet me.

And I came as the man that I am,
not the Messiah others wanted,
in order that the meeting might be honest.

I came so that people would be able
to give to me what they need to give.

A young woman needs to give me her perfume ...
so I take it.

A lonely man needs to give me a meal ...
so I take it.

A cripple needs to give me his hand ...
so I take it as well.

And you, Peter ...
you, at times, need to give me your anger,
your disappointment, and even your despair.

Keep it to yourself, and you'll turn sour.
Give it to your friends and you'll become my enemy.
Give it to me ...
and I'll know that you love me.

But please don't try to protect me from you.
Don't keep back from me
the Peter I came to love and save and summon.

(Pause)

Now, how do you feel?

Peter: *(Coyly)*
A bit embarrassed ...
but a good deal better.

Jesus: Oh, another thing, Peter ...

Peter: Mm-hm?

Jesus: The next time you want to hit me in the solar plexus,
do it in the singular, not the plural.

Peter: What do you mean?

Jesus: Just speak for yourself next time.

Don't say 'we' and 'us'
when you really mean 'I' and 'me'.
Not all the disciples feel paranoid, you know.

Now, what's next?

Peter: I'm going to get something to eat.

Jesus: Are we not both going to get something to eat?

Peter: I was only speaking for myself, Jesus.

Jesus: You're a quick learner, Peter.

Praise music

When the chief priests and scribes saw the wonderful things he did, and heard the boys in the temple shouting, 'Hosanna to the Son of David!' they were indignant and asked him, 'Do you hear what they are saying?' Jesus answered, 'I do. Have you never read the text, "You have made children and babes at the breast sound your praise aloud"?'

Matthew 21: 15–16

Personnel: **Peter**
              Jesus

Peter: Eh ... Jesus ... ?

Jesus: Yes, Peter?

Peter: Do you like music?

Jesus: What kind of music, Peter?
           Folk ...
           Country & Eastern ...
           Hebrew chants?

Peter: I was thinking more in the line of ...
           'praise music'.

Jesus: Where do you hear that, Peter?

Peter: Everywhere, all the time.

It used to be only in the synagogue,
but now people are doing it in their houses.

I even saw a neighbour at it in his garden,
flapping his arms and making a noise
like a sparrow with asthma.

Jesus: Maybe he was just praising God.

Peter: Yes, but God doesn't like praise music.

Jesus: Pardon?

Peter: Exactly …
that's the contradiction …
God doesn't like praise music and you do.

Jesus: And who told you that God doesn't like praise music?

Peter: Amos.

Jesus: A personal conversation was it, Peter?

Peter: No.
It's my favourite verse in his prophecy.
I heard it again last week in the synagogue.

If I remember correctly, it said …
'Stop your noisy songs.
I don't want to listen to your music.'

I'll bet you any money it was praise music!

Jesus: And supposing it was?

Peter: Jesus, if it was, I've got you cornered.

Jesus: How come?

Peter: Simple.
God hates praise music, you love it.

Heaven's going to hear a few arguments when you
return.

Jesus: Peter, since I'm 'cornered',
can I ask you a question?

Peter: Go ahead.

Jesus: If God hates 'praise music' …
why did he let Moses and Miriam dance for joy
after they'd crossed the Red Sea?

Why did he let the Israelites sing in the desert
at the place where water gushed out of the rock?

Why did he allow David not just to sing,
but to dance and sing,
whenever he got saved from an enemy?

Why did he listen to Jonah singing choruses
in the belly of a whale?

Why did …

Peter: *(Interrupting)*
Wait a minute, Jesus,
I thought you only wanted to ask one question!

Jesus: So I did.
I was just putting it in different ways.

If God doesn't like what you call 'praise music',

why does he let so many of his people enjoy it?

Peter: *(Flustered and trying to change the subject)*
Did I just hear Andrew shouting me (calling me)?

Jesus: No.
Andrew's in Capernaum.
And you're in a corner!

Peter: Well, what about Amos?
Did he get it wrong?

Jesus: No, he got it right.

The praise which God accepts
comes from people who have travelled,
from danger to safety
or from darkness to light,
or from despair to hope …

Peter: … or from a ship's hold to a whale's belly?

Jesus: … or from a ship's hold to a whale's belly.

Better a whale that might vomit you up
than a grave at the bottom of the ocean.

And when people sing and shout
after they've been healed,
God accepts that praise too,
because they've travelled from sickness to health
or from rejection to acceptance.

They've got a reason to celebrate.

Peter: But what about Amos?

Jesus: I'm not forgetting Amos.
Amos was pointing to what God loathes and detests ...
praise which comes from the top of the head
and not the heart ...
praise which comes from people
who have never travelled,
who have never left their religious nappies ...
songs which have become a substitute
for serving the poor.

Now, has that solved your dilemma?

Peter: Eh ... yes.

Jesus: You're a great boy for the questions, Peter.

Peter: I take that off my mother.

Come to think of it,
you're a great boy for the singing, Jesus.

Jesus: And I take that off my mother.

When God is hungry

As they left Bethany, Jesus felt hungry and, noticing in the distance a fig tree in leaf, he went to see if he could find anything on it. But when he reached it he found nothing but leaves; for it was not the season for figs. He said to the tree, 'May no one ever again eat fruit from you!'

Mark 11:12-14

Personnel: **Peter**
                      Jesus

Peter: Do plants have souls?

Jesus: Gardener's Question Time, is it, Peter?

Peter: No. The Bible.

Jesus: The Bible?

Peter: Well, the Psalms.

Jesus: The Psalms?

Peter: Well, one of them.

Jesus: Which one?

Peter: The one about the trees clapping their hands.

Jesus: Isaiah.

Peter: No. I'm Peter.

Jesus: Yes, I know you're Peter,
but the quotation doesn't come from the Psalms.
It comes from ...
look, what's this all about anyway?

Peter: Do plants have souls?

Jesus: Why?

Peter: Because if the trees clap their hands to praise God,
they must have souls!

Jesus: But that's poetry, Peter.

Peter: I thought Isaiah was a prophet,
not a poet.
I thought psalms were poetry.

Jesus: Psalms are poetry,
but prophets can write poetry as well.

But what's this all about?
Peter, you're avoiding the issue.
You don't want to ask me
about poets, prophets or psalms.
You want to ask me about something else,
don't you?

Well ... don't you?

Peter: Why did you curse the fig tree?

Jesus: So, that's the real issue ...
Why did I curse the fig tree?

Were you sentimentally attached to it, Peter?

Peter: No ... I just couldn't see any sense in what you did ...
destroying nature,
destroying something with a soul.

Jesus: Let's keep the soul-talk out of it.
Do you remember when I cursed the fig tree?

Peter: Yes ... we'd just walked for about five hours
and my feet were sore
and your stomach was rumbling.

Jesus: That's right.
And I looked for something to eat,
but the fig tree had no fruit to offer.

Peter: But, Jesus, it was the wrong time of year.
It was spring, not harvest.
You don't get fruit off trees in the spring.
It's out of season.

Jesus: Exactly! Exactly!
Peter, what I did to the fig tree was a warning to you
and to all who follow me
that God expects fruit in and out of season.

Peter: What do you mean?

Jesus: I mean that when God is hungry for justice,
he wants it now,
not when diplomats have got their act together.

When God is hungry for peace,
he wants it now,
not after the next war.

When God is hungry for people to know his love,
he won't wait
until the priests have devised a master plan
for evangelism
and the church has its bank balance in the black.

When God is hungry,
the fruit must be produced
whether or not it's the right time.

Peter: That's a tall order, Jesus.

Jesus: God is not a small God, Peter.

Now, what are we going to do until dinner time?

Peter: How about a walk down to the shore?

Jesus: Good ...
and if we walk past the end of your uncle's field,
we might be able to hear the corn 'singing'.

Peter: Isaiah, Jesus?

Jesus: Psalm 65, Peter!

What is Caesar's?

Jesus saw through their trick and said, 'Show me a silver piece. Whose head does it bear and whose inscription?' 'Caesar's,' they replied. 'Very well then,' he said, 'pay to Caesar what belongs to Caesar and to God what belongs to God.'

Luke 20: 23–25

Personnel: **Peter**
               Jesus
               Simon, the Zealot
               Judas

Peter: Jesus ... ?

Jesus: Yes, Peter.

Peter: What's Caesar's?

Jesus: Pardon?

Peter: What is Caesar's?

Jesus: It's a dance hall in Capernaum.

Peter: Come on, Jesus.

Jesus: I think there's another one opening in Bethany.

Peter: Jesus ... what is Caesar's?

I'm not talking about discos.
I'm talking about what you meant when you said,
'Give to Caesar what is Caesar's.'

Simon: Yes, what did you mean, Jesus?

Jesus: Simon, you're interested as well?

Judas: And me.

Jesus: And you, Judas?

Why all this interest?
I say a lot more important things
than 'Give to Caesar what is Caesar's,'
but rarely such a deputation wanting to quiz me.

Judas, what's your interest?

Judas: Well, I look after our money, remember?
And if were going to give to Caesar
every coin which has his face on it,
there'll not be much left.

Jesus: That's true.

But, on the other hand,
if we don't show our respect to the authorities,
we'll not have much going for us.

Simon: On the contrary,
we might have a lot going for us.

Jesus: I thought you might say that, Simon,
but tell us why anyway.

Simon: It's simple.

We live in a country where laws are enforced on us
that we never voted for
by a kind of government we never elected.

Our nation is being put down, walked over.
Why should we pay people to oppress us?

There are a lot of folk waiting
for a group of people like us to say no.

Jesus: Is that not getting politics
mixed up with religion, Simon?

Simon: Listen, Jesus,
it's not just when you rebel.
It's when you side with the authorities
that you get religion mixed up with politics.

Jesus: That's right, Simon.

But what's your interest, Peter?

Peter: I just don't like paying the poll tax.
And it is a poll tax, isn't it?

Simon: Oh yes, it's a poll tax ...
right across the board –
beggar or beauty queen ...
all have to pay
and if you don't ...

Jesus: *(Interrupting)*
Okay, Simon ...
we all know what happens if you don't.
But let's get back to the issue.

I said, 'Give to Caesar what is Caesar's.'

Judas thinks
that might require us
to give everything to the state,
but he'd rather we did that
because they are in control.

Simon thinks
that because we never elected Caesar,
he has no right to our money.

Simon, have you any coins in your pocket?

Simon: One or two ... why?

Jesus: Well, if you believed completely
that we should have nothing to do with the Romans,
you wouldn't have any.

By having Caesar's image in your pocket,
you're admitting
to taking some of the benefits of foreign rule
as well as bemoaning the disadvantages.

Simon: But Jesus!!!

Jesus: Just a minute.
So far you've only concentrated on
one part of what I said.
'Give to Caesar what is Caesar's ...
and to God what is God's.'

(Pause)

Peter: Jesus ...
what if Caesar wants what belongs to God?

(Thinks for a moment)

And what if God wants what Caesar thinks is his?

Jesus: I think that may be an interesting argument
for a few days
or a few weeks
or a few centuries ...

Immaculate

Alas for you, scribes and Pharisees, hypocrites! You are like tombs covered with whitewash; they look fine on the outside, but inside they are full of dead men's bones and of corruption.

Matthew 23:27

Personnel: **Jesus**
              Peter

Jesus: Eh, Peter ... ?

Peter: Yes, Jesus?

Jesus: Did I see you giggling just now
          when I was speaking to the Pharisees?

Peter: No.

Jesus: Peter, my eyes don't deceive me.
          You were giggling when I was speaking to the Pharisees.

Peter: I wasn't giggling
          when you were speaking to the Pharisees.
          I started giggling
          when you were speaking to the lawyers.

Jesus: Why?

Peter: Jesus, you should have seen yourself.
          You were immaculate.

There you were laying into the Pharisees,
telling them
that they didn't know the first thing about justice
– that they were religious show-offs ...

Jesus: *(Interrupting)* Did I say that?

Peter: Well, you said they loved seats of honour
in the synagogue ...
it's one and the same thing.

Then you accused them of being unmarked graves,
and all the time
the lawyers were smirking to themselves in a corner.

And then this upstart thought he'd mix it a bit
and said that he found your language insulting.

But the last thing he expected
was that you'd turn on him
and give him a dose of the same medicine
right between the eyes.

Jesus: *(Interrupting)*
Peter ...

Peter: *(Oblivious)*
... Oh, Jesus,
you really gave them laldie (what for).

You should have seen yourself ...
you grew about six inches taller
and your eyes fixed him in your stare
and your voice went all quiet and husky:

(Mimicking)
'You lawyers ... it's no better for you.

You load people with intolerable burdens
and you don't lift a finger
to help them carry the load ...

Jesus: *(Interrupting)*
Peter ...

Peter: *(Still oblivious)*
'You've stolen the key to the house of knowledge.
You can't go in yourselves
and you make sure nobody else will enter.

You build tombs ...'

Jesus: *(Interrupting)*
Peter ... Peter ...

Peter: Jesus, I was just coming to the good bit.

Jesus: For a lousy fisherman, you make a good actor.

Peter: But, Jesus ...
you were immaculate.

You wiped the floor with them.
I felt like passing round the smelling salts.
They were like jelly.

Jesus: Well, I must admit they did seem a bit shaken.

Peter: Shaken???
Don't sell yourself short, Jesus.
They were decimated!
Did you intend it that way?

Jesus: Well, Peter, unlike you ...
I didn't rehearse my words.
It wasn't till I began that I knew what I had to say.

Peter: You mean ...
all that ... just came out?

Jesus: Yes.

Peter: Immaculate.

Jesus: Is that this week's 'in' word?

Peter: But if it just came to you without any rehearsal,
it *was* immaculate.

Jesus: Well if you say so.

Peter: Is it always like that, Jesus?
Do you never prepare what you are going to say?

Jesus: Peter, all of my life is a preparation
for what I'm going to say.

All the things I hear in the street,
all the people who tell me their secrets,
all the reflecting or arguing about what the Bible says ...
that's all preparation.

Peter: But how come you know exactly what to say
when your back's against the wall ...
like with the Pharisees?

Jesus: Peter,
sometimes it's not until your back's against the wall
that you know what to say
or discover the truth.

If you avoid controversy,
if you speak only to those who agree with you,
you never discover the new things
God has to teach you.

Table talk

It was before the Passover festival and Jesus knew that his hour had come and that he must leave this world and go to the Father. He had always loved his own who were in the world and he loved them to the end. The devil had already put it into the mind of Judas, son of Simon Iscariot, to betray him.

John 13: 1–2

This script is best read before a celebration of the Sacrament, when people are gathered round the altar or table.

The readers, thirteen of them or fewer if some double characters, should be scattered throughout the company. If it is a sizeable gathering, seat them on the circumference. They need not stand to speak unless that would improve their being heard.

If Communion is being celebrated, the celebrant should take the Narrator's part, not that of Jesus. To help the flow of the speech, Jesus should know where everyone is sitting so that he can quickly direct his words to them. It is also helpful to have him positioned centrally with Peter directly within his sight range.

The liturgy of the Sacrament may follow on immediately from the last line or the script may conclude with a hymn, song or chant being sung.

Personnel: **Narrator** *(The Apostle John)*
                      Peter
                      Jesus
                      Andrew
                      Thomas
                      James

Bartholomew
Matthew
Thaddeus
Jim
Philip
Simon
Judas

Narrator: It was at the end of a busy week.

They were sitting at a table in an upstairs room.
Some food had been eaten,
some was still untouched.

The disciples talked and Jesus listened.
Then Jesus talked and the disciples listened.
Then Peter said:

Peter: Jesus ... ?

Jesus: Yes, Peter?

Peter: When are we going to see your Kingdom?

Jesus: Pardon?

Peter: When are we going to see the Kingdom
that you talk about?

I mean, we've been with you for three years now
and, really, we're none the wiser.

I mean ...   I lost my job for you.
I lost all my money.

The only thing I wanted to lose
was my mother-in-law.
But you interfered,
so she's still with us;
and all this time
you've been talking about the Kingdom ...

When are we going to see it?

Jesus: You don't think you've seen it?

Peter: No.
Certainly, you did say
that it would come like a thief in the night ...
and I'm a very sound sleeper.

So, maybe I missed it.

Jesus: Peter, tell me what you remember.

Tell me just one thing you remember
from the time we've been together.

Peter: Eh ...

(Pause)

... eh ... ask somebody else then come back to me.

Jesus: All right ...

Andrew ...
what do you remember?
Just one thing ...

Andrew: The wee (little) boy.

Jesus: Which wee (little) boy?

Andrew: The wee (little) boy with his playpiece (lunch) …
the loaves and fishes.

I remember how you said,
'Have we any food?'
and everybody looked at everybody else.

And then he shouted,
'You can have my playpiece (lunch), mister.'
And everybody laughed.

But you took him seriously …
and the smile was on the other side of our faces.

Jesus: Mm-hm …
what about you, Thomas?

Thomas: The wee (little) girl.

Jesus: Which wee (little) girl, Tom?

Thomas: The wee (little) girl who ran through the crowd.

Remember …
that time you were talking to all the men
and they were eyeing each other up
to see who looked the most religious.

And then the wee girl doddled (wandered)
into the middle of them
with her face and hair covered with strawberry jam.

And her mother was going frantic
in case she was going to cry or wet herself.

And you lifted her up and said,
'Unless you're like this wee (little) girl,
you'll never get into the Kingdom.'

Oh, Jesus, do you remember the Pharisees' faces?

Can you imagine them wearing a bib and rompers?

Jesus: I don't exactly remember you being very enthusiastic
when I asked you to hold her, Tom.

Thomas: Oh, Jesus, I was never good with weans (kids).

Jesus: James, what do you remember?

James: The row you gave John and me
for asking if we could sit beside you in Heaven.

Jesus: Did I really offend you?

James: No …
it's just that we should never have asked that question.
It was my mother who put us up to it.

Jesus: Mothers are sometimes like that, son.

Bartholomew, what about you?

Barth: Oh, Jesus, when are you going to call me Bart
like everybody else?
Bartholomew's my Sabbath name.

Jesus: Sorry … Bart …

Barth: I think I'll always remember the day
when you said that prostitutes and tax collectors
would get first into the Kingdom of Heaven.

Jesus: Why do you remember that?

Barth: Because it shocked me.

I thought you had just said that to annoy people,
until I saw you kneeling down
beside the girl in the square.

And then I remembered what Matthew used to be.

Jesus: Yes, indeed.
Matthew, what do you remember?

Matth: I remember the day you met me.
I remember the day you came by my house
and ate at my table.

If you had stayed at the door and talked,
I would never have listened to you.
I would have thought
you were just another religious maniac.

But you came in and sat down and listened to me.

And I remember the look on the people's faces
when I gave them back the money
I had swindled from them.

I remember the look
when I gave them back twice as much as I had taken.
And I remember how I cried.

I was giving away all my money and I cried,
because I was glad to get rid of it
and make room ... for you.

Jesus: *(Gently)*
I remember that day too, Matthew.

Peter, have you made up your mind yet?

Peter: No, I'm still thinking.

Jesus: All right …

Thaddeus, you never say much …
have you seen much?

Thad: I remember you crying.

Jesus: Why?

Thad: Because I had never seen a man crying …
not in front of women and not in front of other men.

Jesus: Are you afraid of your tears, Thaddeus?

Thad: No … not now.

Jesus: Jim … we haven't heard from you.

Jim: I was just thinking about the day
you told the story about the good Samaritan.

Jesus: What makes you remember that story in particular?

Jim: It put me off being a priest for life.

Jesus: Really?
Remind me to tell you
the story of the prodigal son …
it might put you off drink for life.

Philip, what do you remember?

Philip: I remember the day
you asked the cripple at the side of the lake
if he wanted to get better.

I'm sure that if he could have walked,
he'd have jumped up and booted you.
I mean, he wasn't exactly lying there
to get a sun tan.

Jesus: Sometimes you have to ask hard questions, Philip.

Simon?

Simon: I'm thinking about another time
you were hard on somebody.

You remember the rich young boy
who loved his parents and behaved well,
but he didn't want to part with his money
when you asked him?

You were really hard on him.

Jesus: So I was, Simon.
You wanted me to apologise, didn't you?

You wanted me to run after him and say,
'I didn't really mean it.'

You wanted him to get into the Kingdom of Heaven
as easily as he got into the Rotary Club.

But it's not like that ... is it Judas?

Judas: I don't know.

But if you want to know what I remember,
it happened only on Tuesday
when you let that woman
pour perfume over your head.

Jesus: The gifts of the poor, Judas …
you have to receive the gifts of the poor.

Judas: But that could have been sold for a fortune!

Jesus: I think we've had this argument already.

Peter, have you made your mind up yet?

Peter: The mountain top …
you and Moses and Elijah
having a blether (conversation).

I still think somebody should have built a cairn
or painted a picture of it.

Jesus: Peter, what you saw was for your soul,
not for your display cabinet.

Now, do you remember your original question?

Peter: No … what was it?

Jesus: You asked me
when you were going to see the Kingdom.
And all that you and the others have said
proves to me
that you have at least glimpsed it.

For whoever has seen me has seen the Maker.
And whoever has known what you have known,
has experienced the Kingdom.

It is not of this world,
but it happens in this world.

It happens without you ...
and it happens within you.

It is still to come ...
but it is already here.

The feast has still to be held ...
but the invitations are going out.

Narrator: And then, as they were sitting back,
chewing over his words,
he took a piece of bread ...

The denial

Peter spoke up and said, 'I will never leave you, even though all the rest do!' Jesus said, 'I tell you that before the cock crows tonight, you will say three times that you do not know me.' Peter answered, 'I will never say that, even if I have to die with you!'

Matthew 26: 33–35

This monologue by Peter after his denial of Jesus may be preceded and punctuated, as shown, by a recording of a cock crowing.

Personnel: **Peter**

(Cock crows)

Peter: What did I say?

I didn't mean anything.

I mean, it wasn't that kind of conversation.

I don't mind discussing my faith
with people who know about faith ...
priests ...
ministers ...
you know the sort of people ...

But I mean to say,
when you're just warming your hands at a fire
and some trumped-up chamber maid

starts coming on all holy ...

I mean, you don't know who you're talking to.

I didn't want to encourage her.
I had other things on my mind.

I just said,
'I don't know what you're talking about,'
... and I'd say it again if ...

(Cock crow)

I'll not say it again.

The next time I won't say anything at all.

The next time,
I'll avoid any kind of confrontation,
        any kind of conversation.

The next time,
I won't even shrug my shoulders
or shake my head.

If I do nothing
and say nothing ...
surely that way
I'll neither affirm or deny him ...

The keys

How right Isaiah was when he prophesied about you: 'This people pays me lip-service, but their heart is far from me; they worship me in vain, for they teach as doctrines the commandments of men.'

Matthew 15:9

Jesus and Peter are standing at the gates of Heaven.

Personnel: **Peter**
              Jesus

Peter: Eh ... Jesus ... ?

Jesus: Yes, Peter?

Peter: Eh ... I've got something to tell you.

Jesus: Well, what is it?

Peter: Eh ... I think I've lost the keys.

Jesus: You think you've what???

Peter: I ... I think I've lost the keys.

Jesus: Where did you see them last?

Peter: I think I left them in the door.

Jesus: *(Producing keys)*

Are these them by any chance?

Peter: Oh, Jesus, thank goodness for that.
Where did you find them?

Jesus: I found them where you left them ...
in the door.

Peter: But what were you doing at the door?

Jesus: Oh, I thought I'd just nip outside for a minute
and look at the new arrivals.

Peter: Did they recognise you?

Jesus: Peter, did they ever?
No.
In any case the new arrivals always expect
that everybody here will be dressed
in golden wings and a white nightgown.

So, before I went out,
I changed into a kilt and turban.

Peter: You what???

Jesus: No. I'm just kidding.
I went the way I'm dressed just now.
But nobody recognised me,
even though I knew them all.

And their faces when they got near the pearly gates ...

Peter: Oh, don't tell me.
Gabriel and I have a great time
guessing who's who when they come to the door.

Jesus: Guessing who's who?

Peter: Well, guessing who's what ...
or who *was* what.

Jesus: I'm not any clearer.

Peter: Well, for example, when Presbyterians come ...
I mean when ex-Presbyterians come ...
and you greet them with a smile,
they think there's something wrong.
You would think they expected Heaven
to be a painful place.

And they can't understand
why David sings Psalm 23 to a Jewish tune.
They seem to imagine
that he wrote *Crimond* as well as the words.

Jesus: Really?

Peter: Then there's Methodist women.
They're entirely different.
Whenever you open the door to Methodist women
they try to sell you a ticket for a coffee morning.

Jesus: What about the Catholics?

Peter: Oh, you always know when the Catholics have arrived.
They're hardly in the door
but they're asking for your mother.

Jesus: Aye, she's got a great fan club.

Peter: Then, of course, you get the Orangemen
marching up to the gates singing *The Sash*
and just about swallowing their tonsils
when they see John the 23rd out cutting the grass.

And you can recognise the ministers and priests
right away.
And they try to speak to you in New Testament Greek.
Have you ever heard an Irish priest trying to say
'I'm Father Seamus O'Brien from Cork' in Greek?

Jesus: I can't say I have.

Peter: But, you know, Jesus,
the people I really like to welcome
are those who've had a hard time in life ...

(Pause)

... the ones who were ignored
or turned off by the Church,
but who still remembered you ...
... the ones who looked down
all the time they were on earth,
because nobody ever said, 'Look up,'
... nobody ever said, 'You're important,'
... nobody ever touched them
or listened to their story.

(Pause)

Jesus: I know what you mean.

I met a woman like that the other day.
She was a widow.
She had once done something wrong in her early days.
And though I had forgiven her, nobody else did.

I looked at her eyes
and remembered all the people
who had made her cry.

I looked at her hands
and remembered all the good work she had done
which no one had thanked her for.

I looked into her heart
and remembered how it had been broken
and yet how it had cared and loved.

And I said to her,
'Bessie, there's some people here I'd like you to meet.'

And I was just about to introduce her
to Martha and Lazarus,
when she took my hand and said,
'Jesus, I've had three surprises since I came to Heaven.

The first was finding all the people who are here.
The second was finding all the people who aren't here.
And the third surprise was finding
that I was here myself.'

(Pause)

Peter: Well ... of such is the Kingdom ... eh?

Jesus: Yes ... of such is the Kingdom.

(Pause)

Here, Peter, I'd better be getting back to the top table.
I'll see you later.

Peter: Eh ... Jesus ... the keys?

Jesus: *(Gives them to him)*
Sorry, Peter.

Peter: Thank you, Jesus.

Biblical index of scripts

Some other books from the authors . . .

Stages On the Way
Worship resources for Lent, Holy Week and Easter

Wild Goose Worship Group

Traces Jesus' road to the cross. Helps people to experience the hope, apprehension and joy of Easter as felt by Jesus' friends.

1 901557 11 1 ● Pbk ● 256 pp

Cloth For the Cradle
Worship resources and readings for Advent, Christmas and Epiphany

Wild Goose Worship Group

More litanies, meditations, monologues, scripts, poems, prayers and symbolic actions, this time to help adults rediscover the stories of Christ's birth.

1 901557 01 4 ● Pbk ● 128 pp

States of Bliss and Yearning
The marks and means of authentic Christian spirituality

John L. Bell

Dealing with issues as diverse as private devotion and public debt, John Bell shows that spirituality is not a matter of being in a continual blissed-out state. To experience the heights, one has also to know the depths.

1 901557 07 3 ● Pbk ● 108 pp

A Wee Worship Book
Fourth incarnation

Wild Goose Worship Group

A new, completely revised and expanded edition of this much used and loved book. Geared for participative worship with shared leadership and includes optional methods of scriptural reflection and prayer with symbolic action.

July 1999 ● 1 901557 19 7 ● Pbk ● 128 pp

Songbooks & cassettes ...

There Is One Among Us
BOOK, CASSETTE & CD
Shorter songs for worship
John L. Bell
Short songs, from present-day Scotland and the World Church, that have been sung in prisons, on pilgrimages, at open air festivals, and by cathedral choirs and teenage and in-house music groups. They allow a participation and movement in worship that conventional hymns cannot.
Songbook: 1 901557 10 3 ● Pbk ● 96 pp
Cassette: 21 tracks ● 1 901557 13 8
CD: 21 tracks ● 1 901557 21 9

Love and Anger
BOOK & CASSETTE
Songs of lively faith and social justice
John L. Bell & Graham Maule
Draws on biblical songs of justice, World Church songs of protest and praise, and songs of experience from late twentieth-century Britain.
Songbook: 1 947988 98 X ● Pbk ● 80 pp
Cassette: 1 901557 05 7 ● 19 tracks

For a full catalogue detailing many other books and tapes by these authors and others, please contact:

Wild Goose Publications
4th Floor, Savoy House, 140 Sauchiehall Street,
Glasgow G2 3DH, Scotland
Tel. 0141 332 6292   Fax 0141 332 1090
e-mail: admin@ionabooks.com

Or visit our website www.ionabooks.com
for information on all our products
and the option to order online.

The Iona Community

The Iona Community, founded in 1938 by the Revd George MacLeod, then a parish minister in Glasgow, is an ecumenical Christian community committed to seeking new ways of living the Gospel in today's world. Initially working to restore part of the medieval abbey on Iona, the Community today remains committed to 'rebuilding the common life' through working for social and political change, striving for the renewal of the church with an ecumenical emphasis, and exploring new, more inclusive approaches to worship, all based on an integrated understanding of spirituality.

The Community now has over 240 Members, about 1500 Associate Members and around 1500 Friends. The Members – women and men from many denominations and backgrounds (lay and ordained), living throughout Britain with a few overseas – are committed to a fivefold Rule of devotional discipline, sharing and accounting for use of time and money, regular meeting, and action for justice and peace.

At the Community's three residential centres – the Abbey and the MacLeod Centre on Iona, and Camas Adventure Camp on the Ross of Mull – guests are welcomed from March to October and over Christmas. Hospitality is provided for over 110 people, along with a unique opportunity, usually through week-long programmes, to extend horizons and forge relationships through sharing an experience of the common life in worship, work, discussion and relaxation. The Community's shop on Iona, just outside the Abbey grounds, carries an attractive range of books and craft goods.

The Community's administrative headquarters are in Glasgow, which also serves as a base for its work with young people, the Wild Goose Resource Group working in the field of worship, a bi-monthly magazine, *Coracle*, and a publishing house, Wild Goose Publications.

For information on the Iona Community contact:
The Iona Community, Fourth Floor, Savoy House, 140 Sauchiehall Street,
Glasgow G2 3DH, UK. Phone: 0141 332 6343
e-mail: ionacomm@gla.iona.org.uk; web: www.iona.org.uk

For enquiries about visiting Iona, please contact:
Iona Abbey, Isle of Iona, Argyll PA76 6SN, UK. Phone: 01681 700404
e-mail: ionacomm@iona.org.uk